POP MUSIC STARS

ADAM LEVINE

POP MUSIC STARS

ADAM LEVINE

ARIANA GRANDE

ED SHEERAN

SHAWN MENDES

TAYLOR SWIFT

POP MUSIC STARS

ADAM LEVINE

GREG BACH

MASON CREST
PHILADELPHIA • MIAMI

Mason Crest
PO Box 221876
Hollywood, FL 33022
(866) MCP-BOOK (toll-free)
www.masoncrest.com

First printing
9 8 7 6 5 4 3 2 1
ISBN (hardback) 978-1-4222-4484-5
ISBN (series) 978-1-4222-4480-7
ISBN (ebook) 978-1-4222-7331-9

Library of Congress Cataloging-in-Publication Data

Names: Bach, Greg, author.
Title: Adam Levine / Greg Bach.
Description: Hollywood : Mason Crest, 2022. | Series: Pop music stars |
    Includes bibliographical references and index.
Identifiers: LCCN 2019057466 | ISBN 9781422244845 (hardback) |
    ISBN 9781422273319 (ebook)
Subjects: LCSH: Levine, Adam, 1979–Juvenile literature. |
    Rock musicians–United States–Biography–Juvenile literature.
Classification: LCC ML3930.L38 B3 2021 | DDC 782.42166092 [B]–dc23
LC record available at https://lccn.loc.gov/2019057466

Developed and Produced by National Highlights, Inc.
Editor: Andrew Luke
Production: Crafted Content, LLC

QR CODES AND LINKS TO THIRD-PARTY CONTENT

CONTENTS

KEY ICONS TO LOOK FOR

WORDS TO UNDERSTAND: These words, with their easy-to-understand definitions, will increase readers' understanding of the text while building vocabulary skills.

SIDEBARS: This boxed material within the main text allows readers to build knowledge, gain insights, explore possibilities, and broaden their perspectives by weaving together additional information to provide realistic and holistic perspectives.

EDUCATIONAL VIDEOS: Readers can view videos by scanning our QR codes, providing them with additional educational content to supplement the text.

TEXT-DEPENDENT QUESTIONS: These questions send the reader back to the text for more careful attention to the evidence presented there.

RESEARCH PROJECTS: Readers are pointed toward areas of further inquiry connected to each chapter. Suggestions are provided for projects that encourage deeper research and analysis.

SERIES GLOSSARY OF KEY TERMS: This back-of-the-book glossary contains terminology used throughout this series. Words found here increase the reader's ability to read and comprehend higher-level books and articles in this field.

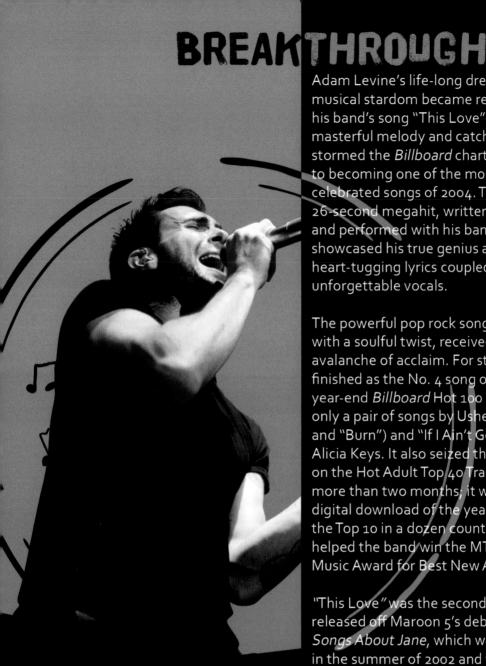

BREAKTHROUGH

Adam Levine's life-long dreams of musical stardom became reality when his band's song "This Love"—with its masterful melody and catchy chorus—stormed the *Billboard* charts on its way to becoming one of the most played and celebrated songs of 2004. The 3-minute 26-second megahit, written by Levine and performed with his band Maroon 5, showcased his true genius at composing heart-tugging lyrics coupled with unforgettable vocals.

The powerful pop rock song, buoyed with a soulful twist, received an avalanche of acclaim. For starters, it finished as the No. 4 song on the year-end *Billboard* Hot 100 list behind only a pair of songs by Usher ("Yeah!" and "Burn") and "If I Ain't Got You" by Alicia Keys. It also seized the No. 1 spot on the Hot Adult Top 40 Tracks chart for more than two months; it was the top digital download of the year; it cracked the Top 10 in a dozen countries; and it helped the band win the MTV Video Music Award for Best New Artist.

"This Love" was the second single released off Maroon 5's debut album *Songs About Jane*, which was rolled out in the summer of 2002 and would go on to sell more than 10 million copies worldwide. They were named Best New Artist at the 2005 Grammy Awards, and in 2006, "This Love" propelled them to capture another coveted Grammy in the category of Best Pop Performance By A Duo or Group with Vocal, fending off challenges by The Killers and Black Eyed Peas.

For Levine, Maroon 5's front man, and his bandmates, this truly signaled the greatness that was to come. The band was in the midst of their first world tour, a 14-month crisscrossing of the globe that began in the fall of 2003 and gathered momentum as "This Love" gained in popularity and took residence at the top of disc jockeys' playlists at radio stations across the country. Maroon 5 performed the song that year on *Saturday Night Live*, won the Choice Rock Track for it at the Teen Choice Awards, and entertained audiences with it while opening shows for big-time performers such as O.A.R., Vanessa Carlton, Counting Crows, Lenny Kravitz, and Sheryl Crow.

"This Love" is where it really all began for the super-talented Adam Levine, who has become one of the most successful and diverse entertainers in music history.

ADAM LEVINE

A HIT AMID THE HEARTBREAK

"This Love" is one of a dozen songs that appears on the *Songs About Jane* album, and each one of them contains at least one reference to a former girlfriend of Adam Levine's named—you guessed it—Jane. Levine wrote "This Love" while in New York right around the time his relationship with Jane Herman had ended, and she was leaving town. The two had met at a gas station and dated for several years. Herman later turned from modeling to writing, including doing pieces for *Vogue* magazine.

ADAM LEVINE

MUSIC VIDEO DEBUTS ON MTV

The music video for "This Love" debuted on MTV's *Total Request Live* program during the first week of 2004. The video was shot at the historic Mack Sennett Studios in Los Angeles, using footage of Maroon 5 playing in a courtyard that was built at the studio. It also features Levine with model Kelly McKee, who was his girlfriend at the time. England's Sophie Muller, who has made videos for Beyoncé, Coldplay, Shakira, and Gwen Stefani, among other big-name stars, directed the video.

"THIS LOVE" IS EVERYWHERE

"This Love" was heard just about everywhere in 2004, from radio and television to the movies—and even video games too. It was featured in the comedy movie *White Chicks* starring Shawn and Marlon Wayans as a pair of FBI agents; it was on the FOX television game show *Beat Shazam* and in a Toyota car commercial; and it could be heard on popular video games such as *Guitar Hero: On Tour, Rock Band 3,* and *Karaoke Revolution.*

 # WORDS TO UNDERSTAND

IMMERSE—involve oneself deeply in a particular activity or interest

MONIKER—name

REJUVENATE—to give new strength or energy to (something)

SUBSEQUENT—coming after something in time, order, or place; following

TRAIPSE—to walk or go somewhere

CHAPTER 1

A STAR IS BORN

DESTINED FOR GREATNESS

Adam Levine's mark on the entertainment industry has been incredibly wide-ranging and mighty impressive. From chart-crushing songs and renowned world tours to 16 seasons of judging on *The Voice* and performing music videos seen by billions, the front man for Maroon 5 has seized superstardom—and shows no signs of letting go anytime soon. While "This Love" punctuated his arrival on the musical landscape and showcased his special gifts, his journey to greatness seemed destined from the beginning.

THE BEATLES' INFLUENCE

Levine was born in Los Angeles on March 18, 1979, to Fredric and Patsy Levine. His dad ran several boutique clothing chains he founded while his mom was an admissions counselor. Levine has a brother (Michael), two half-siblings (Sam and Liza), and a stepsister (Julia). His parents divorced before his eighth birthday. Levine wound up spending the majority of his weeks with his mom and weekends with his dad. It was his mother who cultivated his appreciation for great music early in his life. She loved Simon & Garfunkel, Fleetwood Mac, and The Beatles—a pretty powerful trio of musical acts that helped groom the youngster's musical tastes and style at the beginning.

Levine was born in Los Angeles, where he grew up listening to classic rock, the musical preference of his mother, Patsy.

66 "My mom was a massive Beatles fan. We'd sit in [my mom's] car ... and we'd listen to Abbey Road, and she'd quiz me about which Beatle was singing a certain song."

Levine attended the famed Brentwood School in Los Angeles, an expensive private school that boasts an impressive list of alumni: Emmy Award-winning actress Jennifer Landon; *Titantic* and *Avatar* producer Jon Landau; actor Fred Savage, who starred in *The Wonder Years*; Olympic gymnastics gold medalist Peter Vidmar; and socialite and model Princess Talita von Fürstenberg are among the many noteworthy individuals who have **TRAIPSED** through its hallways. It was on the Brentwood campus where Levine met Jesse Carmichael, Mickey Madden, and Ryan Dusick, who would become important figures in his climb through the music industry when he recruited them to be in his teen band.

BIG DREAMS

By the time Levine reached his high school years, music consumed him and dreams of becoming a rock star grabbed ahold of him and never let go.

Levine's band Kara's Flowers played gigs around Los Angeles and Hollywood.

He devoted all his spare time to writing music, playing guitar, and putting together a teen rock band with his schoolmates in the fall of 1995 that called themselves Kara's Flowers. Nights and weekends quickly evolved into marathon rehearsal sessions where songs were practiced, tweaked, and run through some more. This routine of dissecting notes, altering words, revising vocals, and striving for perfection laid the groundwork for Levine to later become one of the most versatile and beloved entertainers in the world. With Levine handling the vocals along with playing guitar, the group quickly nabbed lots of local attention with their music throughout the Los Angeles area with original songs that included "Captain Splendid," "Soap Disco," "The Never Saga," "Pantry Queen," and "Sleepy Windbreaker."

Soon, Levine's mom was driving the band around town to perform. They got their first official show on September 16, 1995, at Whisky a Go Go, the famed nightclub in West Hollywood. Shortly after, Levine's wide-ranging vocals snared the attention of executives at Reprise Records, who signed the band to its first contract and was a signature moment in Levine's gradual ascension to music stardom.

PLAYING "SOAP DISCO" ON HIT SHOW

Adam Levine got his first taste of the Hollywood spotlight as a teenager, as he and his Kara's Flowers bandmates appeared on an episode of the hit television show *Beverly Hills 90210*. The award-winning show, which debuted in 1990 and ran for 10 seasons, was a prime time teen drama set at fictional West Beverly Hills High School. The show starred Jennie Garth, Tori Spelling, Jason Priestley, Ian Ziering, Luke Perry, and Shannon Doherty. Levine and his group performed their song "Soap Disco" on the episode, which was titled "Forgive and Forget." They performed at the fictional Peach Pit After Dark venue and later released a video of the song.

 Adam Levine and Kara's Flowers perform their song "Soap Disco," the only music video they released under this name.

RELEASE *THE FOURTH WORLD*

Levine and his bandmates went into the studio to put together their first album, and they got to work with legendary producer Rob Cavallo, who has made albums with the Goo Goo Dolls, Green Day, and Michelle Branch, among others. Kara's Flowers debut album *The Fourth World* was released in the summer of 1997.

"Furnishing a home is no different than going into the studio and making music. You want to make sure you've pared down all the extra details so that in the end, every stitch has a context uniquely yours."

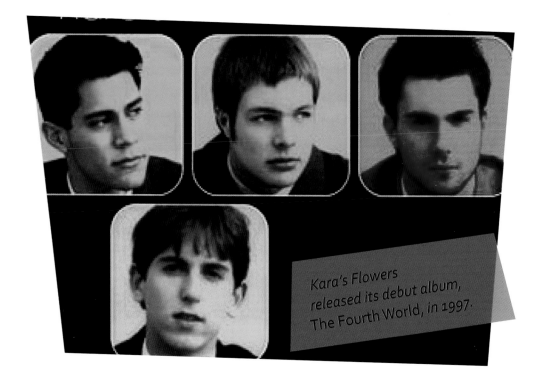

Kara's Flowers released its debut album, *The Fourth World*, in 1997.

With hopes of a best-selling album running high, the band embarked on a late-summer tour. Beginning at Toe's Tavern in Santa Barbara near the end of July, the band played more than 30 tour dates throughout California, Arizona, Washington, Nevada, Minnesota, and New York. They served as the opening act at several stops for bands such as Goldfinger, Reel Big Fish, and the Aquabats. Unfortunately for Levine and Kara's Flowers, the album was a commercial flop and the buzz that had surrounded the band's emergence soon fizzled. When Cavallo exited Reprise Records, executives there who were disappointed in album sales and who also didn't foresee a future of quality music making chopped Levine and Kara's Flowers from their client list.

EASTERN INFLUENCE

Following high school, and no longer having the luxury of a record label, the band broke up and Levine headed east to attend Five Towns College in Long Island, New York. The cozy private college was founded in 1974 and catered to fewer than 700 students looking to pursue careers as musicians, artists, movie producers, and performers. Levine **IMMERSED** himself in a variety of musical disciplines, gaining important knowledge and familiarity with soul, rhythm and blues, gospel, and hip-hop that shaped his thoughts and fueled his passions moving forward.

Levine also began experimenting with different vocal techniques, which in later years would become evident as he began showcasing his expansive range. He was inspired and greatly influenced by the music and life of Stevie Wonder, one of the most admired and respected musicians of the 20th century. Levine also became a big fan of legendary singer, songwriter, and pop icon Bob Dylan; singer Bill Withers, best known for his hit "Lean on Me"; and soul singer Al Green, whose hits included the classic "Take Me to the River."

The legendary Stevie Wonder is one of Levine's influences.

66

"Stevie Wonder is just one of those guys that completely delivers everything that you want to be true about Stevie Wonder. He's an amazing human being, and the fairytale exists with that man."

REFRESHED AND INSPIRED

Levine, **REJUVENATED** from his time in New York, returned to Los Angeles in 2000 full of ideas and inspired to push the accelerator and steer his musical career in a new direction. He reached out to his former bandmates—Madden and Dusick had gone to UCLA while Carmichael went east with Levine—about starting over with a fresh sound, new vibe, and stronger songs. Listening to Levine's passionate pitch, they were all in on giving it another go. Clearly, they recognized the immense talent that resided in Levine and the endless possibilities of where his powerful vocals could lead them. They added James Valentine from the band Square as a second guitarist to round out their group and dove into their work.

Levine handled the bulk of the group's song-writing duties while also fronting the group with his spectacular vocals. They began playing at venues throughout Los Angeles and New York and attracted the attention of executives at Octone Records, a New York-based label. They changed their name to Maroon, then adjusted it again to Maroon 5, and then entered the Rumbo Recorders studio in Los Angeles to record their first album under their new **MONIKER**. Levine wrote or co-wrote each of the dozen songs on the album, which he composed during his time away in New York. They worked with producer Matt Wallace, who had a sparkling background having produced albums with O.A.R. and Train, among other noteworthy groups.

 ## MUSICAL MYSTERY

While Adam Levine was in high school he formed his band Kara's Flowers. The name came about based on a girl all four in the band shared a crush on. The origin of the Maroon 5 name, however, is one of the great mysteries in music—and one that doesn't figure to be solved anytime soon. Levine has been questioned about it on numerous occasions—especially when he appears on popular late-night television talk shows—but he always steers clear of providing an answer. The most popular guess is that since Levine attended Five Towns College, and maroon is one of the school's colors, Maroon 5 was forged through that connection. That is a rumor that has never been substantiated and one Levine is content to remain silent on.

> "It was never my idea to tell anybody. The origin of the (band) name is so bad. It's such a horrendous story that we decided that shrouding it in mystery will make it a better story than the actual story."

SUCCESS STRIKES

The album, *Songs about Jane*, was terrific, and the positive reviews began stacking up around the country. Soon after its mid-2002 release, they began touring with the likes of Michelle Branch and Nikka Costa, and in 2003 did some shows with Sheryl Crow, Matchbox Twenty, John Mayer, and Sugar Ray. In early 2004 the album cracked the Top 20 of the *Billboard* 200 chart and by the end of the year had nudged its way into the Top 10 while becoming the seventh best-selling album of 2004.

Songs about Jane's first single, "Harder to Breathe," gained the album traction as it received plenty of play on radio stations nationwide. It was "This Love," however, that truly announced the arrival of Adam Levine as a super-talent in the industry who was poised to embark on a fantastic career.

Levine was the main songwriter for Kara's Flowers.

By 2004,
Maroon 5's
Songs About
Jane had become
a Top 10 album.

TEXT-DEPENDENT QUESTIONS

1. What was the name of Adam Levine's teenaged band? What hit 1990s television program did they appear on and what was the name of their song they sang on the episode?

2. Which high school did Adam Levine attend? After graduation where did he attend college?

3. What was the name of the first album Levine released with Maroon 5? How did it do?

RESEARCH PROJECT

Adam Levine's first album with *Kara's Flowers* didn't do well commercially, which happens to many artists just starting out in their careers. Put together a list of 10 artists or bands who fared poorly with their first album but then were successful with their **SUBSEQUENT** albums like Levine was with those he released after *The Fourth World*.

 # WORDS TO UNDERSTAND

COLLABORATE—work jointly on an activity, especially to produce or create something

MILLENNIUM—a period of 1,000 years

MOMENTOUS—important; consequential

POIGNANT—arousing deep emotion; touching

SCRUTINIZE—examine or inspect closely and thoroughly

CHAPTER 2
GREATEST MOMENTS

MUSICAL MARVEL

The dawn of the new **MILLENNIUM** in 2000 treated music lovers everywhere to a broad range of remarkable songs and unforgettable performances from some ultra-talented musicians and bands. There was Faith Hill with "Breathe" owning the top pop song of the year to lead off the decade, while Kesha with "TiK ToK" and Lady Antebellum with "Need You Now" closed out the prior decade at the top of the list. In between all the great music being churned out during this timeframe there was also the arrival of Adam Levine and his Maroon 5 band, who jumped smack into the middle of the action by rolling out several top 10 hits that grabbed the attention of the music industry, generated glowing national reviews, produced sold-out concerts, and ignited monster album sales—all accomplished as a direct result of Levine's extraordinary vocals.

In 2002, Levine and his band released their first album (*Songs About Jane*) that went multi-platinum, and five more albums have followed, including 2017's *Red Pill Blues*, which was also the name of the sixth world tour they began in the spring of 2018. The tour hit five continents and concluded on New Year's Eve of 2019 in Las Vegas. Levine's talent is so breathtaking that many of today's top stars want to produce songs with him: in 2005 he appeared on Kanye West's album *Late Registration*, collaborating on the single "Heard 'Em Say"; he was on Alicia Keys' album *Alicia Keys: MTV Unplugged* as part of the cover of the Rolling Stones' song *Wild Horses*; and he performed "Gotten" for a solo album by Slash, the lead guitarist for Guns N' Roses; among countless other projects.

Levine has hosted and performed on *Saturday Night Live* and makes regular appearances on all the major television talk shows, including those hosted by Ellen DeGeneres, Jimmy Fallon, and James Corden. He had a recurring role during the second season of the television series *American Horror Story* and landed a big role in the movie *Begin Again*. Of course, there are also those 16 incredible seasons he did as a judge on *The Voice*, where America saw his huge heart and fun-loving personality shine on a weekly basis.

Levine is a true musical marvel and giant in the industry. Here's a look at some of his biggest moments in a career that overflows with them.

> **"** "I think pain is the best feeling for song writing. You can write good happy songs, but I think the kind of brooding, depressing ones are more effective. They are easier to write when I am impassioned and angry. It is a good way to channel that negative energy."

Levine was honored with a star on the Hollywood Walk of Fame in 2017.

GREATEST MOMENTS

LANDS STAR ON HOLLYWOOD WALK OF FAME

It was a rainy Friday morning on famed Hollywood Boulevard on February 10, 2017, but Adam Levine was all smiles—and with good reason. On this day, in front of family, close friends, and countless fans, he received the 2,601st star on the Hollywood Walk of Fame. Rocker Sammy Hagar, formerly of Van Halen, raved about Levine's talents during his speech at the ceremony. Country superstar Blake Shelton, who was accompanied by his girlfriend and *Voice* co-host, singer Gwen Stefani, also shared touching sentiments about his good friend. Adding to the memorable moment, Levine's wife Behati Prinsloo and four-month-old daughter Dusty Rose were there and posed for a family photo with the star. Levine's star resides in front of Hollywood's Musicians Institute at 6752 Hollywood Boulevard. Levine's speech, delivered over the screams of adoring fans, was filled with thanks to those who impacted his life.

Adam Levine was honored with the 2,601st star on the Hollywood Walk of Fame on Friday, February 10, 2017.

PERFORMS BEATLES' CLASSIC "TICKET TO RIDE"

The date February 9, 1964, remains forever entrenched in American television history, as on this evening The Beatles made their U.S. television debut on *The Ed Sullivan Show*. More than 70 million Americans watched the historical performance that kicked off with "All My Lovin." In honor of that **MOMENTOUS** performance, Adam Levine showed off his guitar-playing skills in 2014 at *The Night That Changed America: A Grammy Salute To The Beatles* show that was held at the Los Angeles Convention Center in 2014. With Beatles legends Paul McCartney and Ringo Starr sitting in the front row, Levine, a life-long Beatles fan, and Maroon 5 performed "Ticket to Ride." Among the others to perform on this star-studded evening were Keith Urban, John Mayer, Brad Paisley, Pharrell Williams, and Imagine Dragons. The special aired on CBS and attracted 14 million television viewers.

Adam Levine and Maroon 5 pay tribute to The Beatles by performing "Ticket to Ride" at The Night That Changed America: A Grammy Salute To The Beatles show in 2014 in Los Angeles.

DEBUTS AS AN ORIGINAL HOST OF THE VOICE

For 16 seasons Adam Levine sat with his back to the stage along with three other celebrity judges, spinning his big red chair around to vie for talented singers to coach on *The Voice*, one of the highest-rated programs in television. A fixture on the reality program since its debut in 2011, his banter with country star Blake Shelton created entertaining subplots as they battled for singers and traded friendly barbs in the process to the delight of viewers. The show has won numerous Emmy Awards. Levine and Shakira have both received a Teen Choice Award for their performances on the show. Gwen Stefani took Levine's place in season 17, which premiered in the fall of 2019, along with Kelly Clarkson, John Legend, and Shelton. The original celebrity coaching cast featured Christina Aguilera, CeeLo Green, Shelton, and Levine. Levine-coached singers won *The Voice* three times—the second most behind Shelton.

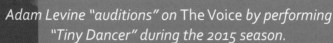

Adam Levine "auditions" on The Voice *by performing "Tiny Dancer" during the 2015 season.*

SINGING WITH STEVIE

One of the biggest musical influences on Adam Levine's career is the legendary Stevie Wonder, so it was a special day for Levine when he got to perform with Wonder at the Benjamin Franklin Parkway in Philadelphia in 2005. The performance was one of many in a series of massive concerts that were held around the world as part of Live 8, an effort aimed at applying pressure on the leaders of the eight richest countries in the world to end poverty worldwide. Besides the United States, concerts were also held in Britain, France, Germany, Italy, Japan, Canada, South Africa, and Russia. The largest concert of them all was in Philadelphia, where Levine performed live in front of an estimated 800,000 people. Other stars that performed in Philadelphia included native son Will Smith, the Black Eyed Peas, the Dave Matthews Band, and Destiny's Child. Levine was introduced to Wonder's music while attending college in New York.

Adam Levine performs with Stevie Wonder at Live 8 in Philadelphia in 2005.

RELEASES SMASH "GIRLS LIKE YOU" MUSIC VIDEO

The power and influence Adam Levine wields in the entertainment industry is undoubtable, and the superstar used it for enormous good in producing one of the most-watched music videos ever. Levine personally reached out to more than two dozen influential and amazing women from all walks of life to appear in his 2018 music video for the Maroon 5 single "Girls Like You," in which he sings with Cardi B. Among those who appear are his good friend, comedian, and television show host Ellen DeGeneres; singers Jennifer Lopez and Camila Cabello; Olympians Aly Raisman in gymnastics and Chloe Kim in snowboarding; activists Trace Lysette and Angy Rivera; and actresses Millie Bobbie Brown and Tiffany Haddish, among others. The video delivers **POIGNANT** messages about female empowerment and the important role women have in society. The video also features Levine's wife Behati Prinsloo and their daughter Dusty Rose.

Adam Levine performs "Girls Like You" with Cardi B.

EMOTIONAL GRAMMY DUET WITH STEFANI

A pair of Grammy Award-winning artists who have worked together as judges on *The Voice* delivered a duet to remember at the 57th Annual Grammy Awards in 2015. On a night filled with star power and dazzling performances, Levine and Gwen Stefani were mesmerizing with their performance of "My Heart Is Open" from Maroon 5's 2014 album *V*. The slow ballad was performed with the singers in classic evening attire—she in a red dress, he in a suit and tie—in front of an orchestra, and it oozed emotion. Neither are strangers to the Grammy stage, with each having won multiple awards. Stefani won two in the mid-2000s with her band No Doubt and one for her collaboration with Eve on "Let Me Blow Ya Mind" while Levine has a trio of Grammy Awards as well, including Best New Artist with Maroon 5 in 2005. Stefani married Blake Shelton, fellow judge on *The Voice*, in 2015.

Adam Levine and Gwen Stefani deliver a live performance at the 57th Annual Grammy Awards in 2015.

PERFORMS ON ACADEMY AWARDS BROADCAST

Adam Levine's first movie role was a big one, as he was cast in the 2013 musical comedy-drama *Begin Again* alongside stars Keira Knightley and Mark Ruffalo. Knightley plays a singer-songwriter by the name of Gretta who is discovered by a struggling record label executive played by Ruffalo. They **COLLABORATE** to produce an album that they record in a variety of spots throughout New York City. Levine plays Gretta's ex-boyfriend who is also a successful musician, so he was clearly a natural for the role. Levine also performed the film's theme song "Lost Stars," which earned numerous award nominations, including an Academy Award nomination for Best Original Song. "Lost Stars" was performed live for the first time on the season finale of *The Voice*'s seventh season by Levine and his team member Matt McAndrew, and he performed it at the 87th Annual Academy Awards with Maroon 5.

Adam Levine performs "Lost Stars," the theme song from the movie Begin Again, *which earned an Academy Award nomination for Best Original Song in 2015.*

SHIRTLESS AT THE SUPER BOWL

A global audience watched Adam Levine and his Maroon 5 bandmates take the stage for one of the biggest honors in music—headlining the halftime show at Super Bowl LIII at Mercedes-Benz Stadium in Atlanta in 2019. Rapper Travis Scott and Atlanta native Big Boi also performed. The band opened the show with "Harder to Breathe," one of its early hits, and then performed a number of fan favorites, including "This Love" and "Girls Like You." Midway through "Moves Like Jagger," the closing song, Levine ditched his shirt in a move that was heavily **SCRUTINIZED** and debated on social media. Past halftime shows have featured Justin Timberlake, Lady Gaga, Bruce Springsteen & The E Street Band, Coldplay, Beyoncé, Katy Perry, Missy Elliott, Lenny Kravitz, Bruno Mars, the Red Hot Chili Peppers, Madonna, Nicki Minaj, The Who, Tom Petty and the Heartbreakers, Prince, the Rolling Stones, Paul McCartney, and U2, among others.

Adam Levine and Maroon 5 performed at halftime of Super Bowl LIII in Atlanta in 2019.

By the end of 2019, Levine and Maroon 5 had six hit albums and had completed six world tours.

TEXT-DEPENDENT QUESTIONS

1. What *Beatles'* classic did Adam Levine and Maroon 5 perform in 2014 at *The Night That Changed America: A Grammy Salute To The Beatles* show in Los Angeles?

2. What prestigious award was Adam Levine recognized with on February 10, 2017? Who are the other performers who attended the ceremony and shared thoughts about Levine?

3. Who did Adam Levine sing a duet with at the 2015 Grammy Awards? What song did they sing?

RESEARCH PROJECT

Writing songs that eventually wind up on the albums of top artists requires a lot of skill, and likely some luck on occasion too. Choose three of your favorite bands or artists and delve into where the lyrics for their songs come from. Do they write all their own songs? Do they have certain writers they lean on more than others? Have they ever used a random submission from a writer?

WORDS TO UNDERSTAND

CONNOISSEUR—one who enjoys with discrimination and appreciation of subtleties

HAIL—come from; have one's home or origins in a place

HEINOUS—an evil or monstrous act

LIEU—place; stead

PAPARAZZI—freelance photographers who aggressively pursue celebrities for the purpose of taking candid photographs

CHAPTER 3

BEHIND THE CURTAIN

WHEN THE SPOTLIGHT DIMS

Fronting one of the most popular bands in the world gobbles up massive amounts of time: there are songs to compose, albums to produce, global tours to perform, non-stop television and magazine interviews to do, red carpet events to attend, charity obligations to fulfill, and so on. For Adam Levine, all these demands pulling on his time come with the territory of being one of the biggest names in the entertainment industry. His life isn't all music, all the time, however. He isn't under the glare of the spotlight, or in the lens of a **PAPARAZZO'S** camera, every hour of the day. Levine has a family he cherishes and a variety of hobbies and interests that he enjoys that provide a well-rounded life.

Levine married Victoria's Secret model Behati Prinsloo in 2014.

MARRIED TO AN ANGEL

Years ago, Levine had reached out to Victoria's Secret Angel Behati Prinsloo, wondering if she would be interested in appearing in one of Maroon 5's upcoming music videos that was in the works. While she was unable to squeeze the project onto her calendar at the time—she's an in-demand model who has worked with top-of-the-line designers like Versace, Ralph Lauren, and Alexander Wang and graced the covers of leading fashion magazines—the two began exchanging emails and gradually a connection was forged. In 2012, with an opening in her schedule and an interest to meet Levine in person, Prinsloo flew to Los Angeles to appear in a music video the band was recording for "One More Night." Prinsloo, who **HAILS** from Namibia, a country in southern Africa, and Levine had chemistry from the start and began dating shortly thereafter. Their first appearance on the red carpet came a few months later in New York City at the GQ Gentleman's Ball.

After a year-long engagement the couple got married on July 19, 2014, at Flora Farms in Los Cabos, Mexico. It was a massive affair attended by numerous A-list celebrities, including actor Robert Downey Jr., Jason Segel from the hit show *How I Met Your Mother*, and Victoria's Secret models Erin Heatherton and Candace Swanepoel, among others. Actor and comedian Jonah Hill, whose numerous movie credits include *Forgetting Sarah Marshall* and *Superbad*, officiated the ceremony. Stevie Nicks and Sublime with Rome performed at the reception. In **LIEU** of wedding gifts, the couple asked for charity donations and later honeymooned in South Africa.

FAMILY FOCUS

Levine and his wife are the proud parents of two daughters: Dusty Rose, born September 21, 2016, and Gio Grace, born February 15, 2018. Since deciding not to return to *The Voice* for a 17th season, Levine has been savoring life at home with his family. During November 2018 Levine's wife posted a rare family photo on her Instagram page of her and Adam pushing their daughters on a swing set with the caption "Thankful."

 Adam Levine and Maroon 5 perform "Sugar" during the 2015 season of The Voice.

"I'm obsessed with them. I know that's a good thing, because they're my children. I genuinely adore them in a way that I never knew I could adore any little person."

HAPPY HOME

Levine's family owns a $31.95 million, six-bedroom, seven-bathroom house in Pacific Palisades, California, a noted refuge for celebrities. The nearly 9,000 square foot home is on a three-acre lot and features a swimming pool. Hollywood stars Ben Affleck and Jennifer Garner had previously owned the home. The move marked a busy few months of both looking and selling. They put two homes on the market near the end of 2017: a house in Holmby Hills for $18 million and another in Beverly Hills for $15.9 million. They had lived in the five-bedroom Holmby Hills house for only a few months. They were in the midst of a large renovation but after learning that they had a second child on the way, they ditched the project.

GOLF FANATIC

Besides spending time with his family, one of Levine's favorite pastimes is teeing it up on the golf course. An avid player, he squeezes in rounds whenever he can while at home and when he's crisscrossing the globe on tour with Maroon 5. He even savors the solitude of spending hours on the driving range pounding buckets of balls to work on his swing.

> "When I do have time to play or to grind, which is my favorite activity, I basically will hit more golf balls than any person on the planet earth. I will hit thousands of balls a day and wouldn't even think twice about it."

HACKING IT WITH HANK

Several years ago, he competed on *The Haney Project*, Golf Channel's

Former boxing champion Sugar Ray Leonard was one of Levine's playing partners in a charity golf program in 2012.

hit series that features four celebrities who strive to improve their golf skills under the coaching of legendary golf instructor Hank Haney, who is best known for the work he did coaching Tiger Woods. During the series Levine competed against boxer Sugar Ray Leonard, chef Mario Batali, and model and actress Angie Everhart. Each participant received $20,000 to donate to a charity of their choice and the winner received an additional $20,000.

On the season finale in Cabo San Lucas, Mexico, following eight episodes of intense instruction and practice on all aspects of the game, Haney chose Levine as the most improved of the four. Levine donated the $40,000 he pocketed to the Teen Impact Program at Children's Hospital in Los Angeles, which provides support for children, teens, and young adults battling cancer and blood diseases.

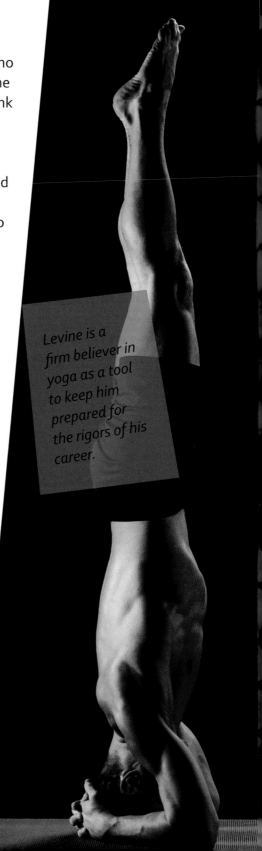

Levine is a firm believer in yoga as a tool to keep him prepared for the rigors of his career.

MOVES ON THE MAT

Being the headliner of global concert tours is physically draining and mentally taxing, as the pressure to perform at a high and entertaining level accompanies Levine every time he steps on stage. Years ago, he discovered yoga as the perfect

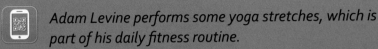

Adam Levine performs some yoga stretches, which is part of his daily fitness routine.

antidote to help keep in shape for performing all the moves he puts his body through during shows, as well as to relax and free his mind before going out to perform in front of thousands of people. There are many forms of yoga, though the basics of the art involve performing various moves and poses along with relaxed breathing and meditation.

Levine typically spends about an hour before going on stage going through a variety of moves, including the sirsasana (headstand), tadasana (mountain pose), sarvasana (corpse pose), and bhujangasana (cobra pose), among others. Levine continually touts the benefits yoga has had on his life, and he has shared several Instagram posts raving about how it has helped alleviate the aches and pains that accumulate while traveling and performing for grueling periods of time that often keep him away from home for many months at a time.

> "It has had such a profoundly positive impact on my life over the years. I have never been pretzel-ish or particularly flexible. And my practice is riddled with mistakes and imperfections. Which is precisely what makes it so powerful. Striving to do better while simultaneously remaining satisfied with where I am. It's much larger than I am. I just tag along for the ride. Pretty cool. So ... thanks yoga. You're awesome."

ROCKING THE ROLEXES

Whether it's on the red carpet, on stage, in a photo shoot, or driving around town, Adam Levine sports an impressive array of Rolex watches on his left wrist. One piece he is spotted wearing more than most is the Rolex Submariner. This watch, which was unveiled in 1956, first gained notoriety on the wrist of Sean Connery in several James Bond movies, including *Dr. No, From Russia With Love, Goldfinger,* and *Thunderball.*

INKED UP

Five days after the horrific attacks on September 11, 2001, in which the Twin Towers were destroyed in New York City and 2,977 people were killed, Levine got his first tattoo. Wanting to display something peaceful in response to the **HEINOUS** acts, he chose a dove that was inked on his upper left bicep. It turned out to be the first of many tattoos that Levine has gotten through the years. He has a massive tattoo on his back of a mermaid cradling a skull, with crashing waves, a ship, and swallows in the background. The scene took six months to complete. In recognition of his ties to California he has "Los Angeles" inked on his upper right bicep and "California" in big capital letters arcing over his belly button on his stomach. He has "Noah" on the right side of his abdomen, which is his mom's maiden name and also his middle name, and he has "Mom" on his right wrist. He had the letters for "True Love" tattooed across his fingers after he got married to Behati Prinsloo. Among his other work he has a tiger on his right arm, a shark on his side and an eagle on his ribcage.

> **"** "Tattoos wind up being this strange road map or narrative over the years. They always remind me of this long, weird, awesome journey life has been."

PASSION FOR PORSCHES

Levine is a long-time **CONNOISSEUR** of classic cars, and he is always tinkering with his collection by purchasing new models and at times selling others. A self-proclaimed Porsche fan, his collection features Porsches, Ferraris, Cadillacs, and American muscle cars. An uncle who was always driving a variety of different Porsches whetted his taste for classic cars. Once Levine crossed the threshold of stardom and his bank account swelled, he purchased a collector's Porsche—a 1958 Speedster—and hasn't slowed down since in stockpiling an impressive array of vehicles.

Levine's first of several tattoos was chosen in response to the terrorist attacks in New York, Washington, D.C. and Pennsylvania in 2001.

Levine and his wife can often be spotted tooling around Beverly Hills, Hollywood, and Los Angeles in one of his vintage cars, often his black 1956 Porsche 356 Speedster convertible. In the spring of 2018, Levine test drove the unreleased electric Mission E Porsche. Footage of his test drive was featured on Porsche's official YouTube channel. He recently unloaded a 1955 Mercedes-Benz 300 SL Gullwing coupe at an RM Sotheby's auction in Fort Lauderdale, Florida, that fetched a whopping $1.115 million. Levine had owned the car for a half dozen years and it had more than 50,000 miles (80,467 kilometers) on it.

Levine has a weakness for Porsche sports cars.

TEXT-DEPENDENT QUESTIONS

1. What is Adam Levine's favorite hobby? What is the name of the television show he appeared on to compete against others who share his passion for this activity? How did he fare?

2. What types of cars does Adam Levine collect?

3. How many children does Adam Levine have? What are their names?

RESEARCH PROJECT

Adam Levine has an impressive vintage car collection, a popular hobby among many music stars. See how many other entertainers you can find who have vintage car collections and rank their collections in order of who you believe has the most impressive sets of wheels in their garages.

 # WORDS TO UNDERSTAND

ACOUSTIC—of, relating to, or being a musical instrument whose sound is not electronically modified

ACTIVISM—the policy or action of using vigorous campaigning to bring about political or social change

CHRONIC—having an illness persisting for a long time or constantly recurring; having a bad habit

IMMIGRANT—a person who comes to live permanently in a foreign country

PLIGHT—a dangerous, difficult, or otherwise unfortunate situation

CHAPTER 1

BRAND ADAM LEVINE

A LIFE OF IMPACT

One of the most brilliant pieces of social **ACTIVISM** to appear in recent years was delivered through the creative genius of Adam Levine in a gripping 4-minute 30-second music video for the hit "Girls Like You" in which he sings with Cardi B. The video, released in the summer of 2018, delivered an important message on female empowerment and featured a stunning cast of amazing women who are impacting the world in never-before-seen ways. Within the first week of its release it had more than 45 million views on YouTube and has now been seen a jaw-dropping 2.4 billion times on that website.

For Levine, the father of two young daughters, the project connected him to the **PLIGHT** of women and the video speaks volumes about his character and genuine passion for what is happening on the planet. It is also another in a long line of big-hearted efforts he has spearheaded to make a difference in the lives of others. From donating time and money to help children battling cancer, to speaking out about Attention Deficit Hyperactivity Disorder (ADHD) to help those who are dealing with the condition like he is, to using the power of his huge followings on social media to share important messages, Levine's

Levine's first
daughter, Dusty
Rose, was born
in 2016.

list of touching deeds is long and mighty impressive. This is especially true of the "Girls Like You" music video that seized the world's attention.

FEMALE EMPOWERMENT

Levine worked with video director David Dobkin on the masterpiece, which took a week to shoot and six months to edit together. It begins with Levine alone at a microphone on a rotating platform, when suddenly female icons begin showing up one by one dancing and lip-synching behind him. There's Ellen DeGeneres, Jennifer Lopez, Mary J. Blige, Camila Cabello, Alex Morgan, Danica Patrick, and Sarah Silverman. There's Olympic gymnast Aly Raisman wearing a T-shirt with the phrase "Always Speak Your Truth;" Minnesota politician Ilhan Omar, the first Somali-American Muslim legislator to be elected to office in the United States; **IMMIGRANT** rights activist Angy Rivera with the phrase "Undocumented Unafraid Unapologetic" on her T-shirt; and so many more women leading lives of impact.

One of the more poignant moments in the video that overflows with them occurs at the end of the song when Levine embraces his wife Behati Prinsloo, who is cradling their daughter Dusty Rose.

SPEAKS OUT ON SOCIAL MEDIA

Levine is heavily followed on social media, with more than 12 million followers on Instagram, nearly 10 million on Facebook, and more than eight million on Twitter. He uses his voice on these platforms in a variety of ways. Along with the typical posts announcing concert venues, new album releases, and tour bus shots, Levine frequently speaks out on important societal issues.

On Twitter he encouraged people to donate to support the Red Cross Disaster Relief Fund when Hurricane Dorian ravaged the Bahamas and Carolinas. He also has engaged with young fans fighting serious health issues. When the brother of a high school sophomore in Tennessee awaiting heart surgery posted footage of the sick teen performing Maroon 5's "She Will Be Loved" from the intensive care unit with his dad playing guitar, Levine was quick to respond with encouraging words that the youngster was thrilled to receive.

ADHD

Millions across the country have been diagnosed with Attention Deficit Hyperactivity Disorder (ADHD) and Levine is one of them. He learned he had the **CHRONIC** condition—which is characterized by impulsive behavior, inattention, and hyperactivity—during his teen years. With proper treatment both children and adults with ADHD can live successful and productive lives. Levine has been an active proponent of encouraging people to learn more about the condition and what can be done to help those dealing with it. Back in 2011 he helped launch the Own It initiative, which is supported by

Levine has struggled with ADHD since he was a teenager.

both the Attention Deficit Disorder Association and Children and Adults with Attention Deficit/Hyperactivity Disorder. He also starred in a Public Service Announcement.

Levine has spoken often about how as a child he didn't understand what he was dealing with, and once he got to high school he wasn't surprised to discover he had ADHD because he had such difficulty focusing in class. He has used his powerful voice to encourage those with ADHD to learn about the symptoms and speak with a doctor. That's exactly what Levine did: when he recognized it was affecting his career like it impacted his performance in school, he sought out a doctor to learn more about how best to approach the condition.

RAISES AWARENESS FOR TESTICULAR CANCER

Years ago, Levine posed nude to help raise awareness for prostate and testicular cancer and encourage men to check and be aware of the signs and symptoms associated with the disease. The photos appeared in an edition of *Cosmopolitan UK* magazine and generated plenty of publicity, which was the purpose in shifting the spotlight to a disease that often doesn't get much attention compared to many others.

Levine has supported testicular cancer awareness as one of the many causes he champions.

TESTICULARCANCER
AWARENESS

Through concerts and special events, Levine and Maroon 5 have raised hundreds of thousands of dollars for the Teen Impact Program at Children's Hospital Los Angeles.

Adam Levine does impressions of famous entertainers on The Tonight Show Starring Jimmy Fallon.

DELIVERS BIG FOR TEEN IMPACT PROGRAM

Levine and his Maroon 5 mates have been key and long-time supporters of the Teen Impact Program at Children's Hospital Los Angeles, which provides psychosocial support services for preteens, teens, and young adults battling or surviving cancer and blood diseases. The program reaches more than 1,200 preteens, adolescents, and young adults every year—at no cost to patients and their families.

The program was founded by Dr. Aura Kuperberg, who has been vocal in her gratitude for what Levine and Maroon 5 have meant to the success of the program and their ability to provide assistance at no cost. They have raised hundreds of thousands of dollars for the program through concerts and special events, along with sharing their time through one-on-one and group music lessons for patients, visiting hospitalized patients, donating

Maroon 5 donated their $500,000 appearance fee for playing the Super Bowl LIII halftime show to Big Brothers Big Sisters of America.

guitars for music lessons, providing opportunities for children with cancer and blood diseases to meet and play with the band, and even playing **ACOUSTIC** sets during Teen Impact group meetings. When Levine won $40,000 during his season on *The Haney Project* on The Golf Channel, he donated it to the Teen Impact Program.

SUPER DONATION

During the swarm of media attention that accompanied the lead up to Super Bowl LIII, Levine shared how having the chance to deliver the halftime performance at the big game at Mercedes-Benz Stadium in Atlanta was a dream come true. What he and his Maroon 5 bandmates chose to do with their hefty performance fee made even more dreams come true for countless others: they donated their $500,000 payday to Big Brothers Big Sisters of America.

MIGHTY MOMS

The drive for helping others runs in Levine's family. His mom Patsy Noah and Sharon Feldstein, the mom of actor and director Jonah Hill, started YourMomCares in 2018. The foundation is dedicated to helping underprivileged children. Shortly after forming it they raised $50,000 for the Children's Health Fund, a group that provides assistance to children dealing with mental illness. YourMomCares works with a variety of charities that focus on helping children. Other celebrity moms to join their efforts include Guadalupe Rodriguez, mother of Jennifer Lopez; Alicia Keys' mom Terria Joseph; and NBA star Chris Paul's mom Robin Paul.

222 CLOTHING LINE

Levine's lucky number is 222—it is tattooed on his left forearm—and it is the name of the clothing line he launched in 2013. The collection, which is designed for both men and women, features jeans, T-shirts, jackets, belts, scarves, silk dresses, and knit tops. There are also baseball hats paying

Among Levine's many tattoos is "222", which he considers his lucky number and is the name for his clothing line. He also honors his birth state with "CALIFORNIA" spelled out across his abdomen.

homage to his California roots with "Los Angeles" displayed on them. The clothing line is featured in Kmart stores and on the Shop Your Way website.

Levine's father, Fred, was also part of the venture. His dad had been involved in the retail industry for decades and ran a chain of specialty clothing stores in Los Angeles called M. Fredric.

THE SCENT OF SUCCESS

Levine has lent his name to a variety of products through the years. He teamed up with New York-based ID Perfumes to develop his signature line of cologne and perfume in 2013 that featured unique packaging: the bottles were in the shape of a microphone, with a weighted cap in silver mesh and a black stem. The fragrances were made available at Macy's.

Throughout his career Levine has won a bunch of awards and been labeled many things, and in 2017 he picked up another title: Fragrance Ambassador. YSL Beauty, owned by the popular L'Oreal brand, bestowed the title for the launch of Y, a new cologne for men.

Levine has also collaborated with First Act to create the First Act 222 Guitar, which was designed to his specifications and was sold in Target stores; and he's appeared in commercials for the acne product Proactiv, detailing his struggles with breakouts during his teenage years.

MORE 222

Relying on those lucky numbers once again, Levine launched his own record label in 2012 called—you guessed it—222 Records. The first artist he got to sign was Matthew Morrison, who starred in the hit television series *Glee*. Other artists to join the label included singer and songwriter Rozzi Crane, who collaborated with Maroon 5 on the *Hunger Games* soundtrack that debuted at No. 1 on *Billboard's* Top 200 chart; Tony Lucca, who was a finalist on *The Voice*; and singer Diego Boneta, who starred in the movie *Rock of Ages*. In the summer of 2014, 222 Records forged a distribution partnership with Interscope Records. It released the soundtrack to *Begin Again*, Levine's first film, and months later released *V*, Maroon 5's fifth studio album.

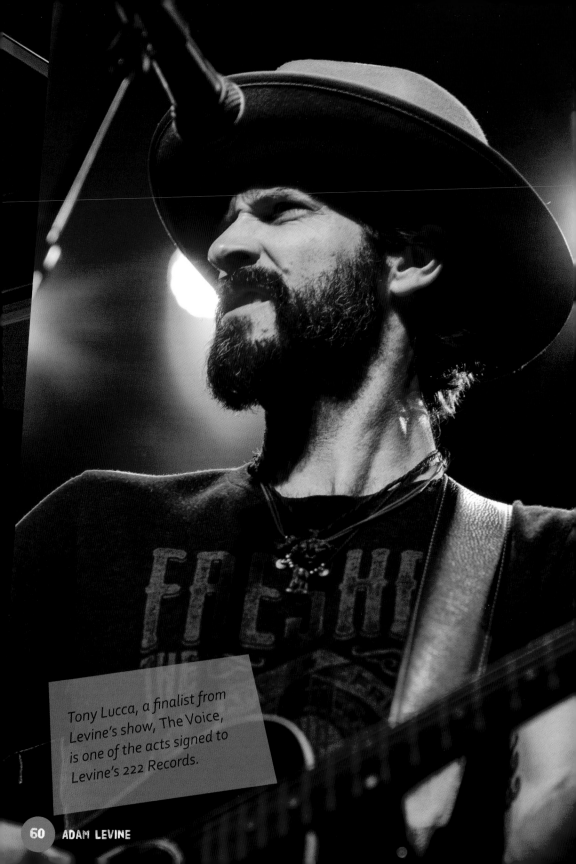

Tony Lucca, a finalist from Levine's show, The Voice, is one of the acts signed to Levine's 222 Records.

TEXT-DEPENDENT QUESTIONS

1. What condition was Adam Levine diagnosed with as a teenager? What is his message to adults who are dealing with it just like he continues to?

2. How many followers does Adam Levine have on Twitter? How has he used that platform to help others?

3. When Adam Levine posed mostly nude in *Cosmopolitan UK*, what diseases was he hoping to draw attention to?

RESEARCH PROJECT

Adam Levine does heart-warming work for the Teen Impact Program at Children's Hospital Los Angeles. Choose a cause that has meaning to you in your community and research how you and your friends could follow in Levine's footsteps by helping out on occasion throughout the year.

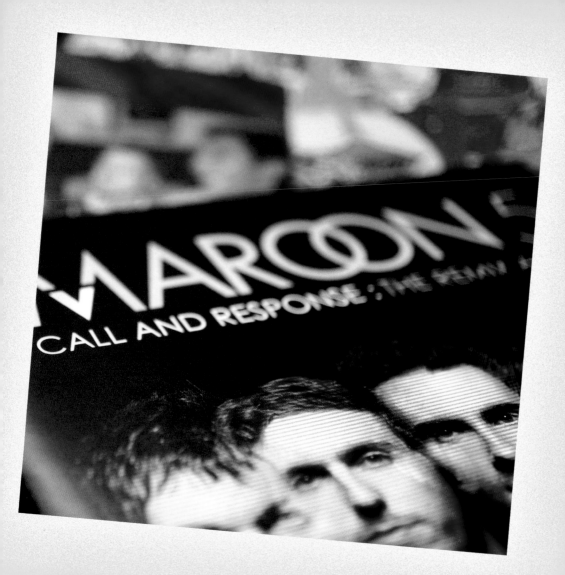

 # WORDS TO UNDERSTAND

DABBLING—working or involving oneself superficially or intermittently, especially in a secondary activity or interest

ECHELON—a group of individuals or entities at a particular level or grade in an organization or field of activity

SHREWD—given to wily and artful ways or dealing

VIRTUOSO—a person highly skilled in music or another artistic pursuit

CHAPTER 5
MODERN MEGASTAR

VOCAL VERSATILITY

When Adam Levine stepped onto the massive stage at London's Wembley Stadium in the summer of 2019, a throng of 80,000 people anxiously waited for this **VIRTUOSO** of vocals to take them on a musical journey. Veering between rock, rhythm and blues, love ballads, and more, the super-talented Levine and his Maroon 5 band have been delivering these must-see performances across the globe for two decades now. On this evening, at the Capital Summertime Ball featuring 19 different acts, it was another masterful performance by one of the industry's premier entertainers and downright fabulous singers.

Since the release of its first album in 2002, Levine has taken the band to heights and places the members never imagined. Millions of fans have been soaking up every delicious verse belted out. Levine's vocals have dominated the radio airwaves with a variety of hits, from "She Will Be Loved" to "Moves Like Jagger," and "Sugar." His fingerprints are all over some of the most prestigious awards the industry has to offer. He is the recipient of three Grammy Awards, two Billboard Music Awards, a pair of American Music Awards, an MTV Video Music Award, a World Music Award and was *Variety's* 2018 Hitmaker of the Year.

Levine is a three-time Grammy Award winner with Maroon 5.

ANALYZING THE ALBUMS

In 2005, Maroon 5 picked up two Grammy Award nominations for Best New Artist (they beat rapper Kanye West to win it) and Pop Performance by a Group for "She Will Be Loved." Their second album, *It Won't Be Soon Before Long*, arrived on music shelves in the late spring of 2006. "Makes Me Wonder," the lead single, earned a Grammy, while two other singles— "Won't Go Home Without You" and "If I Never See your Face Again"—earned Grammy nominations. "Makes Me Wonder" jumped from No. 64 to No. 1 on the *Billboard* Hot 100 chart, the biggest climb ever at the time.

WEDDING CRASHERS

The biggest day in the lives of several brides and grooms in Los Angeles was made even more memorable, courtesy of Adam Levine and his Maroon 5 bandmates. On December 6, 2014, the band drove across the city, popping in on countless weddings to collect footage for the music video for their single "Sugar." The surprise visits produced screams and cheers at venues throughout the city and provided memories for couples and those attending the nuptials to last a lifetime.

Maroon 5's third album, *Hands All Over*, was pieced together in Lake Geneva, Switzerland, with well-known producer Robert John "Mutt" Lange, who had reached out in the hopes of overseeing the project. Levine and his band spent two grueling months putting the album together, as their days were filled with writing and re-writing songs. The group's "Moves Like Jagger" single with Christina Aguilera debuted at No. 8 on the *Billboard* Hot 100 and raked in worldwide acclaim as the ninth-best digital single of 2011.

> "He worked me harder than anyone ever has. I would come in with a finished song, and he'd say, 'That's a good start. Now strip it down to the drums and start over.' The coolest thing about (Mutt Lange) is that not only has he been a huge, legendary producer, but he also is a legit, serious writer."

In 2012, the *Overexposed* album was rolled out, landing at No. 2 on the U.S. *Billboard* 200 chart; two years later Maroon 5 unveiled its fifth studio album *V*; and in 2017 they released *Red Pill Blues*.

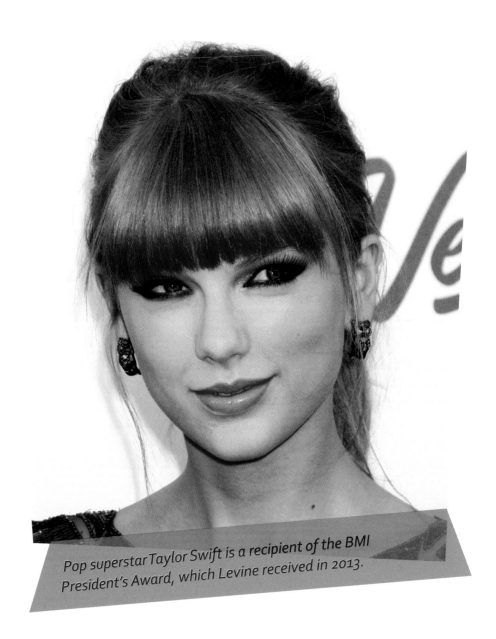

Pop superstar Taylor Swift is a recipient of the BMI President's Award, which Levine received in 2013.

Adam Levine appears on The Ellen DeGeneres Show *in 2019.*

WONDERFUL WRITER

In 2013 Levine received the BMI President's Award for his contributions as a songwriter at the 61st Annual BMI Pop Awards in Beverly Hills, California, joining past winners Taylor Swift, Gloria Estefan, Pitbull, and country music legend Willie Nelson. Then the following year Levine was named the BMI Songwriter of the Year for his hits "Daylight," "Love Somebody," and "One More Night."

DYNAMIC DUETS

Levine hooked up with hip hop rockers Gym Class Heroes on their single "Stereo Hearts," which was released in the summer of 2011 and shot to No. 4 on the Hot 100 chart. Levine became the first artist to have a No. 1 Top 40 hit with Maroon 5's "Moves Like Jagger" while simultaneously having another Top 10 hit on the *Billboard* chart with "Stereo Hearts." Plus, he occupied the No. 1 spot again with "Locked Away," a song by R. City on which Levine was featured in 2015. He's also done guest vocals with this impressive cast: Kanye West, Jason Derulo, 50 Cent, and Alicia Keys, among others.

SCREEN STAR

Levine made his television acting debut on the second season of *American Horror Story* in 2012 on the FX network, where he plays a newlywed and—spoiler alert— things take a nasty turn at the hands of a serial killer. He made a cameo as himself during the 12th season of the *Family Guy* and wound up on the big screen with a hefty role in the feature film *Begin Again*. Levine also performed the film's theme song "Lost Stars," which earned an Academy Award nomination for Best Original Song. He co-wrote "Go Now," which is featured in the 2016 movie *Sing Street*, and he had roles in the 2017 movie *Fun Mom Dinner* starring Molly Shannon and the 2018 comedy movie *The Clapper* featuring Ed Helms and Amanda Seyfried. Levine was tapped to host *Saturday Night Live* in 2013, where one of his skits involved comedian Jerry Seinfeld and actress Cameron Diaz.

Levine appeared with Saturday Night Live alumnus Molly Shannon in the 2017 movie Fun Mom Dinner.

DEALING IN DEATH

Amid all his success, Levine has also faced heartbreak. He suffered a tragic loss when his manager and childhood friend Jordan Feldstein died unexpectedly in December 2017 from a blockage of an artery in his lungs and a blood clot in his leg. Feldstein is the older brother of actor Jonah Hill. Feldstein had played a huge role in the success of Levine and Maroon 5, and his death created a huge void in the lives of all those who loved him deeply and who leaned on him for guidance and direction in the chaotic and difficult-to-navigate music industry.

> **"It was a tragedy foisted upon us and far and away one of the saddest moments of our lives, and personally of mine. This is a kid I've known since we were in diapers. He was one of the most important people in my life from a very early age."**

POKING FUN AT POKÉMON

When the Pokémon Go craze was running rampant in 2016—the mobile game where mostly teens used their cell phones to travel around and locate and capture virtual creatures—Maroon 5 jumped into action. In their music video for their song "Don't Wanna Know," the group appears in bug-like costumes resembling Pokémon creatures and are chased and captured by teens armed with their smartphones. The video features several well-known celebrities, including actors Ed Helms and Vince Vaughn, comedian and actress Sarah Silverman, and former NBA champion Shaquille O'Neal.

Levine makes all the musical decisions for Maroon 5.

While grieving over the loss of Feldstein, Levine also understood the importance of plugging ahead, something he knew his good friend would want those around him to do. Levine brought Feldstein's business partner Irving Azoff and manager Adam Harrison into the fold to help manage the band. All decisions regarding Maroon 5's music are made by Levine, and with good reason—he has a **SHREWD** mind and golden touch to go with those spectacular vocal cords.

"I've got a beautiful family, a beautiful wife, two beautiful babies, and I've got money in the bank, and I'm really happy with my career and my output and the person that I've become and the person that I hopefully will stay."

EXECUTIVE PRODUCER OF SONGLAND

After being in front of the camera all those years on *The Voice*, Levine is **DABBLING** with behind-the-scenes responsibilities as one of the executive producers for the television show *Songland* that debuted on NBC in the spring of 2019. Each week songwriters work with mentors from the music industry with the winner having the chance to have their song recorded by a famous special guest artist. The 11-episode first season featured numerous stars, including John Legend, Meghan Trainor, OneRepublic, Macklemore, Kelsea Ballerini, and Ester Dean, who wrote "What's My Name" for Rihanna, "Super Bass" for Nicki Minaj, and "Firework" for Katy Perry.

"It's so authentic. It's a fascinating look into how it goes down, and I can assure you that is how it goes down. At least major aspects of it are represented on the show, and it's amazing."

Levine was a judge on the hot television program The Voice *for 16 seasons.*

OPENING ACT

Also in 2019, Maroon 5 was the first act to perform at the brand new Hard Rock Live venue, located at the Seminole Hard Rock & Casino in Hollywood, Florida, which is near Miami. It was a special appearance by the band, as Maroon 5 typically sells out stadiums, so the 6,500 fans that packed the new theatre for the show were thrilled.

Adam Levine and Maroon 5 team with Christina Aguilera to sing "Moves Like Jagger" at the 39th Annual American Music Awards.

FABULOUS AT FORTY

Levine turned forty in March 2019, already having accomplished so much in his spectacular career. From the hit music as a solo artist, as well as elevating Maroon 5 into the upper **ECHELON** of great bands of the era as the front man for the group, his vocal versatility continues to amaze and delight audiences worldwide. Plus, Levine's impact on the entertainment landscape, from 16 seasons on television's *The Voice* to appearing on the big screen, is undeniable. Adam Levine's rise from a teenager with big dreams of music stardom to surpassing everything he could have ever imagined achieving is one of the most amazing journeys in entertainment history. Millions of fans can't wait to see what he does next.

NBC Experience Store

the
VOi
SEASON
PREMIERE FEB 27 | MO

Levine's fellow judges for the 2012 season of the Voice were Blake Shelton, Gwen Stefani and Alicia Keys.

TEXT-DEPENDENT QUESTIONS

1. Name two movies Adam Levine has appeared in.

2. What award did Adam Levine receive in 2014 that recognized his brilliance as a songwriter?

3. Who passed away in 2017 that had a significant impact on Adam Levine's life and is someone he misses dearly?

RESEARCH PROJECT

Adam Levine is one of many entertainers who does outstanding charity work to help others. Which solo artist or band today impresses you the most with their efforts away from the stage to help others? Put together a list of 10 examples to back up your case for who is doing the best work.

SERIES GLOSSARY OF KEY TERMS

Acoustic: of, relating to, or being a musical instrument, whose sound is not electrically enhanced or modified.

Album: a collection of audio recordings released together as a collected work.

American Music Awards: an annual music awards show, generally held in the fall, where artists win fan-voted awards in various categories. It is the first of the Big Three music award shows held annually (the others being the Grammy Awards and the Billboard Music Awards).

Billboard Music Awards: an honor given out annually for outstanding chart performance by *Billboard*, a publication and music popularity chart covering the music business. The Billboard Music Awards show had been held annually since 1990, but went dormant from 2006–2011. They are now held annually in May and is the third of the Big Three music award shows.

Chart: a ranking of music (songs, albums, etc.) according to popularity during a given period of time.

Choreography: the sequence of steps and movements in dance, especially in a staged dance.

Genre: a category of artistic composition, as in music or literature, characterized by similarities in form, style, or subject matter.

Grammy Awards: awards presented by The Recording Academy to recognize achievements in the music industry. The annual presentation ceremony features performances by prominent artists and an awards presentation. The Grammys are the second of the Big Three major music awards held annually.

Indie artist: a musician who produces independently from major commercial record labels or their subsidiaries.

Multi-platinum: having sold two million or more copies of an album.

Vocal range: the measure of the breadth of pitches that a human voice can phonate. Its most common application is within the context of singing, where it is used as a defining characteristic for classifying singing voices into groups known as voice types.

FURTHER READING

Bentley, Bill. *Smithsonian Rock and Roll Live and Unseen.* Washington: Smithsonian Books, 2017.

Govan, Chloe. *Maroon 5: Shooting for the Stars.* London: Omnibus Press, 2013.

Green, Dylan. *Piano and Keyboard for Beginners: How to Play Famous Piano Songs and Read Music.* Independently Published, 2019.

Maroon 5. *Easy Guitar with Notes & Tab.* Milwaukee: Hal Leonard Publishing, 2015.

Maroon 5. *Maroon 5 V.* Milwaukee: Hal Leonard Publishing, 2015.

INTERNET RESOURCES

http://iam222.com
The official website of Adam Levine, featuring videos, music, news, photos, and more of the entertainment superstar.

https://www.maroon5.com
The official website of the band *Maroon 5*, featuring all the latest news, information on tour dates and tickets, concert videos, photos, merchandise, and more.

https://www.etonline.com
The Entertainment Tonight website has the latest celebrity news, photos, and videos.

https://ew.com
The Entertainment Weekly website has the latest news about TV shows, movies, and music, as well as exclusive behind-the-scenes content from the entertainment industry.

https://extratv.com
Extra features the latest celebrity and entertainment news and gossip, photos, videos, games, music, movies, star sightings, and more.

https://people.com
The official website of *People* magazine has the latest news about celebrities, royals, music, and TV, along with photos and videos.

INDEX

AUTHOR BIOGRAPHY

Greg Bach is the author of more than 20 books on sports and music. He is a proud graduate of Michigan State University, where he majored in Journalism. He resides in Greenacres, Florida.

PHOTO CREDITS

Pgs. 1, 54, 70: Andre Luiz Moreira/Shutterstock.com, pgs. 3, 34: Debby Wong/Shutterstock.com, pg. 6: ChristinaR/Wikimedia Commons, pg. 8: Everett Collection/Shutterstock.com, pg. 9: Donna Lou Morgan, U.S./Wikimedia Commons, pg. 10: FashionStock.com/Shutterstock.com, pg. 12: Chris Rubino/Shutterstock.com, pg. 13: Gabriele Maltinti/Shutterstock.com, pg. 16: Public Domain/Wikimedia Commons, pg. 17: Kobby Dagan/Shutterstock.com, pg. 19: PrinceOfLove/Shutterstock.com, pgs. 20, 25, 36, 56: Featureflash Photo Agency/Shutterstock.com, pg. 22: A.RICARDO/Shutterstock.com, pgs. 24, 50, 66, 68, 72: Kathy Hutchins/Shutterstock.com, pg. 38 JStone/Shutterstock.com, pg. 41: Jaguarps/Dreamstime.com, pg. 42: LightField Studios/Shutterstock.com, pg. 45: Ken Tannenbaum/Shutterstock.com, pg. 46: BlaineT/Shutterstock.com, pg. 48: Jaguar PS/Shutterstock.com, pg. 52: ibreakstock/Shutterstock.com, pg. 53: james weston/Shutterstock.com, pg. 58: Antonio Scorza/Shutterstock.com, pg. 60: J.A. Dunbar/Shutterstock.com, pg. 62: Kraft74/Shutterstock.com, pg. 64: DFree/Shutterstock.com, pg. 74: Leonard Zhukovsky/Shutterstock.com

EDUCATIONAL VIDEO LINKS

Pg. 15: http://x-qr.net/1LLm, pg. 26: http://x-qr.net/1LG6, pg. 27: http://x-qr.net/1Hu1, pg. 28: http://x-qr.net/1L6p, pg. 29: http://x-qr.net/1KPU, pg. 30: http://x-qr.net/1Kg4, pg. 31: http://x-qr.net/1LwT, pg. 32: http://x-qr.net/1Kww, pg. 33: http://x-qr.net/1LYj, pg. 40: http://x-qr.net/1L58, pg. 43: http://x-qr.net/1K4c, pg. 55: http://x-qr.net/1LJ3, pg. 67: http://x-qr.net/1M71, pg. 73: http://x-qr.net/1KmZ